My Easter

Activity and Sticker Book

BLOOMSBURY
Activity Books
NEW YORK LONDON NEW DELHI SYDNEY

Draw silly shoes on the birds.

Decorate the plant pots.
Add flower stickers.

3

Add faces, arms, and legs to some
of the patterned eggs.

4

Doodle and sticker your own patterns
on the blank eggs.

5

6

Find Charlie Chick hiding in the eggs!

Continue the pattern across the page.

You will find stickers to help you.

Color and add matching sticker eggs to the tree.

Help the rabbits find the Easter basket.

a

b

Match the shadows on this page to the bunnies on the opposite page.

c

d

e

f

Find the bunny stickers to match the shadows.

Find and color 8 chicks,
4 rabbits, and all the eggs.

Now color the flowers and birds.

17

Using the dots as a color guide,
color the rabbit and the basket.

18

Decorate the hats
using the flower and
ribbon stickers.

chick, and rabbit decorations to the string.

Draw yourself and your friends
hunting for eggs in the garden.

Spot the differences between the carousel on this page and the page opposite.

There are 8 to find.

Use stickers to decorate the eggs.

a

b

c

Which jigsaw piece completes the picture?
Find the sticker.

27

Draw the other half of the missing rabbits.
Use stickers to dress some rabbits.

Draw lines between the matching chicks.
Color the large chick in the center.

Color in the doodles. Add more doodles and stickers to this page.

Draw a picture of the Easter Bunny, and make a list of names for all the rabbits on this page

_____

_____

_____

_____

_____

_____

_____

Page 3

Pages 4–5

Page 9

More→